Dino-Soaring

Written and illustrated by Steve Smallman

"PARP!"

"Oh no!" said Stretch. "What a smell!"

It was no fun being a small apatosaurus in a herd of smelly, grown-up apatosauruses!

Stretch looked up at the pterodactyls.
"If only I could fly!" he said.

"I know!" said Stretch.
"I *will* try to fly!"
He took a big leap off a rock,
flapping his legs like mad.

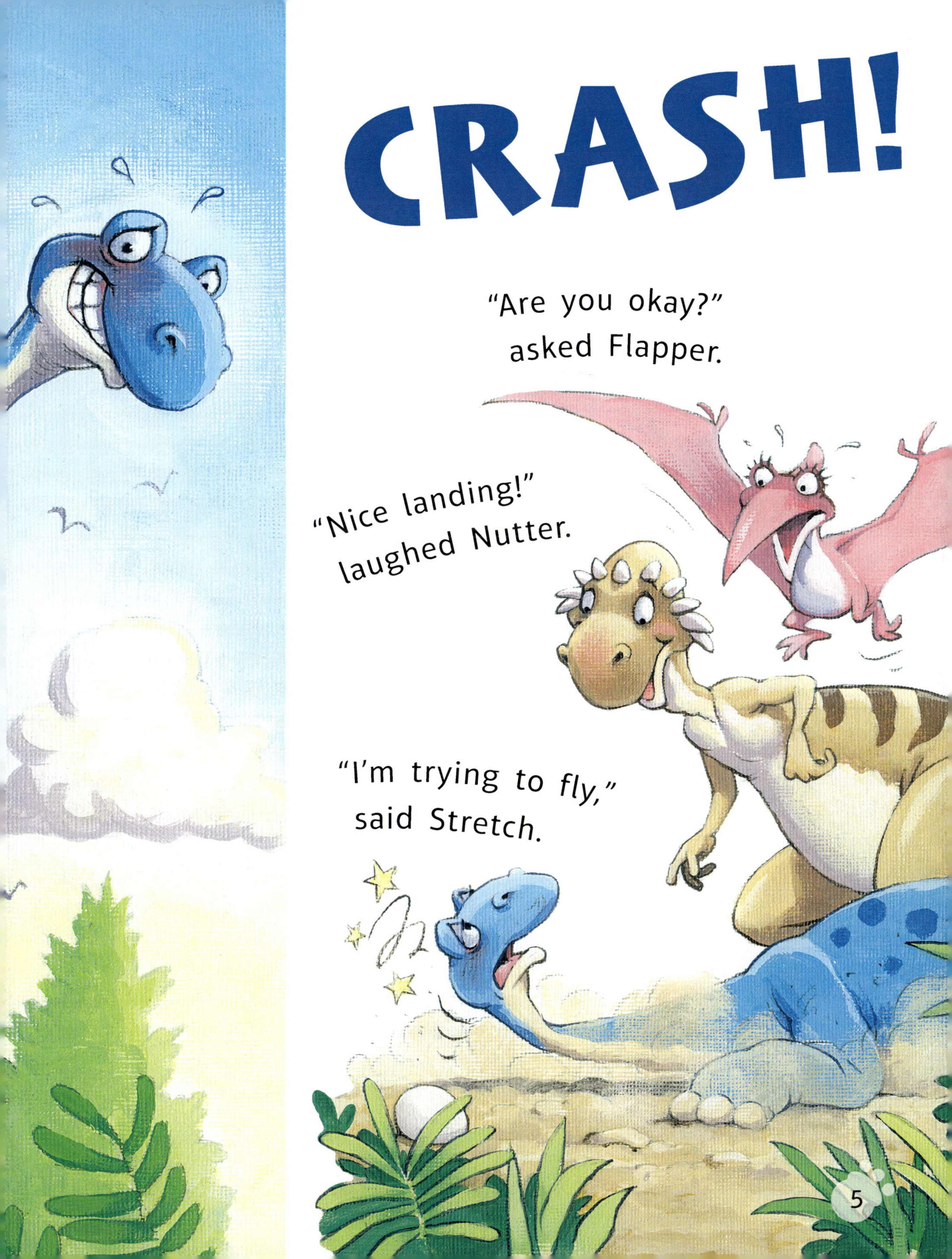

CRASH!

"Are you okay?"
asked Flapper.

"Nice landing!"
laughed Nutter.

"I'm trying to fly,"
said Stretch.

"But you can't fly.
You don't have wings!" said Nutter.

"Let's *make* you some wings!"
said Flapper.

Nutter pushed down some trees.

Stretch tore off the leaves.
Flapper tied them together with some vine.

Soon Stretch's wings were ready!

Flapper gave Stretch some flapping lessons.

Nutter showed him how to land on his head!

Then Stretch got up onto a big rock.

"Jump!" called Nutter. "You can do it!"

Stretch took a big jump.

Wheeeeeeeeeeee...

Flap,
flap,
flap ...

CRUMP!

Some pterodactyls were giggling at Stretch.
"Don't just sit there," shouted Flapper. "Help!"
So they did!

Flapper and the pterodactyls cut some bits of vine and put them under Stretch's tummy and legs.

"Now," called Flapper. "**LIFT!**"

The pterodactyls lifted Stretch into the air.

"I'm flying!"
Stretch shouted.

The other apatosauruses looked up at Stretch.

They didn't spot the huge tyrannosaurus rex creeping up to attack them.

Luckily Stretch saw it and ...

a big dollop of apatosaurus poo
hit the T-rex in the face!

The T-rex gave a roar and ran off,
trying to wipe its face with its little T-rex arms.
Stretch, the flying apatosaurus, was a hero!